Destroyers

by Michael Green

Consultant:

Jack A. Green

Naval Historical Center

CAPSTONE
HIGH/LOW BOOKS
an imprint of Capstone Press
Mankato, Minnesota

Capstone High/Low Books are published by Capstone Press
818 North Willow Street • Mankato, MN 56001
http://www.capstone-press.com

Library of Congress Cataloging-in-Publication Data
Green, Michael, 1952–
    Destroyers/by Michael Green.
    p. cm. — (Land and sea)
    Includes bibliographical references and index.
    Summary: Discusses the history, weapons, missions, and possible
future of Navy destroyers.
    ISBN 0-7368-0041-7
    1. Destroyers (Warships)—United States—History—Juvenile literature.
2. United States—History, Naval—Juvenile literature. [1. Destroyers (Warships)]
I. Title. II. Series: Land and sea (Mankato, Minn.)
V825.3.G74 1999
623.8'254'0973—dc21

                                                              98-3634
                                                                CIP
                                                                 AC

Editorial Credits
Matt Doeden, editor; James Franklin, cover designer and illustrator;
    Sheri Gosewisch, photo researcher

Photo Credits
Archive Photos, 38
Department of Defense, 6, 30
UPI/Corbis-Bettman, 14
U.S. Naval Historical Center, 26
U.S. Navy, 4, 8, 11, 12, 17, 19, 22, 25, 28, 32, 34, 37, 40, 43, 47

Table of Contents

Chapter 1

Destroyers

Destroyers are long, slender warships. The U.S. Navy uses destroyers to protect its other warships and to attack enemy ships. Destroyers mainly attack enemy submarines. Submarines can travel underwater and on the water's surface. Destroyers also attack enemy aircraft.

Destroyers are light and small. This allows them to be fast. Destroyers carry only small amounts of fuel. This helps destroyers remain as light as possible. Navy members call destroyers tin cans.

Destroyers are fast warships.

Destroyers are lighter than most warships.

Size and Speed

People use displacement to measure the sizes of ships. A ship pushes water away from itself while afloat. Displacement is the weight of that water. The smallest modern destroyers have

displacements of 8,300 tons (7,530 metric tons). The largest destroyers have displacements of 9,900 tons (8,981 metric tons). The largest destroyers are much lighter than most other warships. Large warships

Destroyer crews launch torpedoes out of torpedo tubes.

such as aircraft carriers have displacements of almost 100,000 tons (90,720 metric tons).

Modern destroyers are either 466 feet (142 meters) long or 563 feet (172 meters) long. This is smaller than most warships. The small size of destroyers allows them to travel more quickly than most warships.

People measure the speeds of ships and boats in knots. One knot equals 1.15 miles (1.85 kilometers) per hour. The fastest modern destroyers can reach speeds of 35 knots. This is about 40 miles (65 kilometers) per hour.

Weapons and Armor

Destroyers have powerful weapons. They carry machine guns, torpedoes, missiles, and depth charges.

A torpedo is an explosive that travels underwater. Destroyer crews launch torpedoes out of torpedo tubes.

A missile is an explosive that can fly long distances. Destroyer crews launch missiles at enemy aircraft and warships.

A depth charge is a metal can filled with explosives. Destroyer crews drop depth charges into the water to attack enemy submarines. Depth charges can weigh as much as 600 pounds (272 kilograms).

Some destroyers have anti-aircraft weapons. Crews use these guns and missiles to shoot down enemy aircraft. Destroyers also have guns that can shoot down enemy missiles in flight.

Few destroyers have armor. Armor is a protective metal covering. Destroyers must be fast. They often are in battles with small, fast ships. Heavy armor would slow down destroyers. But destroyers without armor do not last long against heavy enemy fire.

Range

Destroyers cannot travel far before they need to refuel. Destroyers usually carry enough fuel to last about two days. Large amounts of fuel would slow down destroyers.

During wartime, destroyers usually stay near their fleets. A fleet is a group of warships under one command. Destroyers get their fuel from other ships in their fleets.

Destroyer crews drop depth charges into the water to attack enemy submarines.

Mast

Radar

Gun

Bridge

966

Hull

Chapter 2

Early Destroyer History

Navies built the first destroyers in the late 1800s. They built destroyers to attack torpedo boats. Torpedo boats were small, fast boats that launched torpedoes at large warships.

The British Navy built the first torpedo boats in 1877. This was 13 years after a Scottish scientist invented the torpedo.

Torpedo boats were a danger to large warships. Large ships were not as fast as torpedo boats. They could not change direction as easily. Many large warships could not protect themselves against torpedo boats.

Navies built the first destroyers to attack torpedo boats.

During the 1890s, navies built fast, powerful warships to destroy torpedo boats. They called the ships torpedo boat destroyers. Early torpedo boat destroyers could travel at about 30 knots. They carried guns and torpedoes.

Navies built larger torpedo boat destroyers during the early 1900s. Navies used fewer torpedo boats. Navies began using their torpedo boat destroyers against enemy warships. Torpedo boat destroyers became known as destroyers.

By the 1930s, navies used destroyers for more than just battle. Destroyers escorted large warships. To escort means to travel with and protect. During World War II, destroyers carried crews on scouting missions. The crews watched for enemy ships and aircraft.

World War I Destroyers

The U.S. Navy had 52 destroyers before World War I (1914–1918). It built more destroyers

Torpedo boat destroyers became modern destroyers like this one.

during the early years of the war. The navy had more than 200 destroyers when the United States entered World War I in 1917.

By World War I, U.S. Navy destroyers were able to attack large warships. Destroyers launched torpedoes to attack enemy ships. Their torpedoes traveled at about 35 knots. Destroyers had to be close to enemy ships before they could attack. The enemy ships could escape if destroyers were too far away. Destroyers used their speed to surprise enemy ships.

Destroyer crews learned how to attack at night. Enemy ships could not easily spot destroyers then. Crews created smoke screens during day attacks. Enemies often could not spot destroyers through the smoke.

But enemies still sunk many U.S. destroyers. Destroyers had no armor. They could not last long in battles against large warships. Many early destroyers sank.

The U.S. Navy built new destroyers for World War II.

Preparing for World War II

The U.S. Navy stored many of its destroyers after World War I. It did not have enough money to keep them in service. The U.S. Navy did not begin building new destroyers until the

World War II Naval Battles of the Pacific Ocean

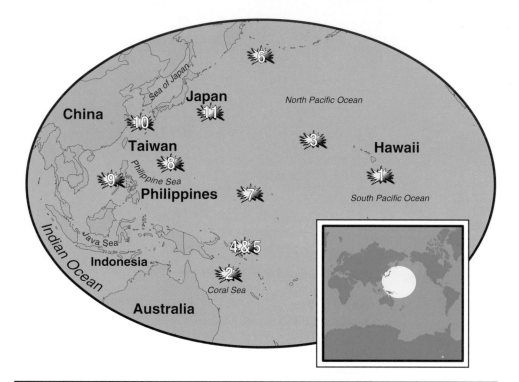

1. Pearl Harbor,
   Dec. 7, 1941
2. Battle of the Coral Sea,
   May 4-8, 1942
3. Battle of Midway,
   June 3-6, 1942
4. Guadalcanal Campaign,
   Aug. 1942 to Feb. 1943
5. Northern Solomons Campaign,
   Feb. 22, 1943 to Nov. 21, 1944
6. Battle of the Komandorski Islands,
   Mar. 26, 1943

7. Truk Attack,
   Feb. 17-18, 1944
8. Battle of the Philippine Sea,
   June 19-20, 1944
9. Leyte Campaign,
   Oct. 17, 1944 to July 1, 1945
10. Sinking of the *Yamato,*
    Apr. 7, 1945
11. Destruction of the Japanese navy,
    July 10 to Aug. 15, 1945

1930s. That was when the Japanese military began building many new warships.

U.S. military leaders knew there might be a war against the Japanese military. The navy ordered many new destroyers.

The Japanese military attacked the U.S. Naval base at Pearl Harbor, Hawaii, on December 7, 1941. The attack brought the United States into World War II (1939–1945). Manufacturers quickly built destroyers for the war.

Fletcher Class Destroyers

The Fletcher class destroyer was the most common U.S. destroyer during World War II. The United States built 175 Fletcher class destroyers for the war. These warships first entered the war in 1942.

The navy built Fletcher class destroyers for speed. Their powerful engines gave the destroyers a top speed of 40 knots. Fletcher

Fletcher class destroyers were 376 feet (115 meters) long.

class destroyers were small. They were 376 feet (115 meters) long and 39 feet (12 meters) wide. They had displacements of about 2,800 tons (2,540 metric tons).

Fletcher class destroyers carried about 273 people. They could travel up to 9,000 miles (14,484 kilometers) without refueling. They traveled in groups of four called divisions.

Sumner Class Destroyers

Navy leaders saw a need for larger destroyers as World War II continued. They wanted destroyers that could carry more guns. The navy created Sumner class destroyers to carry six guns. Previous destroyers had carried only five. The navy built 70 Sumner class destroyers.

Sumner class destroyers were 376 feet (115 meters) long and more than 40 feet (12 meters) wide. Their displacement was 2,890 tons (2,622 metric tons). They could reach speeds of about 35 knots.

Gearing Class Destroyers

Many navy leaders were unhappy because they felt Sumner class destroyers were too small. Navy leaders wanted destroyers that could carry more fuel. So the navy built a new class of destroyer called the Gearing class.

Gearing class destroyers were 376 feet (115 meters) long and 41 feet (12 meters) wide. They carried about 350 people. They had

Gearing class destroyers traveled at speeds of up to 34 knots.

displacements of 3,160 tons (2,867 metric tons) and traveled at speeds of up to 34 knots.

The U.S. Navy built more than 100 Gearing class destroyers. But it used few of these ships in the war. Most were not ready before the United States and its allies won the war in 1945.

Chapter 3

Recent Destroyer History

The U.S. Navy had more than 600 destroyers after World War II. The navy scrapped many of the destroyers that were in poor condition.

The Soviet Union began building many submarines during the 1950s. Navy leaders worried that the United States would need new destroyers to battle the submarines. The navy rebuilt some destroyers. It also created new classes of destroyers.

The navy created new classes of destroyers during the 1950s.

Rebuilt Destroyers

The U.S. Navy rebuilt more than 100 World War II destroyers during the 1950s. The navy removed most of the destroyers' anti-aircraft guns. The old guns could not shoot down new jet airplanes. The navy armed the rebuilt destroyers with more powerful torpedoes, missiles, and guns. It also gave some destroyers room to carry small helicopters.

The navy divided its rebuilt destroyers into two groups. One group of destroyers had weapons to destroy submarines. These ships kept the name destroyers. The other group had weapons that could destroy submarines, aircraft, or other warships. This group of destroyers became known as guided missile destroyers. People on these ships control guided missiles while the missiles are in the air.

Guided missile destroyers have weapons to destroy submarines, aircraft, and other warships.

Kidd class destroyers are guided missile destroyers.

New Destroyers

The navy began building Forrest Sherman class
destroyers in 1955. Forrest Sherman class
destroyers had displacements of more than
4,000 tons (3,629 metric tons). They were 407
feet (124 meters) long and 45 feet (14 meters)
wide. Their top speed was about 33 knots.

The navy built all 18 of its Forrest Sherman class destroyers partly with aluminum. Aluminum is a light, silver-colored metal. The Forrest Sherman class destroyers were larger than previous destroyers. But they remained light and quick because they were made of aluminum. The U.S. Navy began using aluminum to build most of its new destroyers.

The navy built 23 Charles F. Adams destroyers from 1958 to 1964. These destroyers were similar to Forrest Sherman class destroyers. Charles F. Adams class destroyers were slightly larger than Forrest Sherman class destroyers. They carried more weapons.

Kidd Class Destroyers

During the 1970s, manufacturers built four Kidd class destroyers for Iran. This was a new class of guided missile destroyer. But Iran's government changed before manufacturers finished building the destroyers.

Spruance class destroyers are still the most common class of destroyer today.

Manufacturers did not sell the destroyers to Iran's new government.

The U.S. Navy bought the four Kidd class destroyers instead. These destroyers are still in service. They carry modern weapons such as guided missiles, torpedoes, guns, and depth charges.

Kidd class destroyers have displacements of 9,574 tons (8,686 metric tons). They are 563 feet (172 meters) long and 55 feet (17 meters) wide. They carry crews of about 339 people. Their top speed is 35 knots.

Spruance Class Destroyers

The U.S. Navy began building Spruance class destroyers during the 1970s. It built them to replace the destroyers from the 1950s. The navy built 31 Spruance class destroyers. These destroyers became the navy's most common class. They are still the most common class of destroyer today.

Spruance class destroyers have displacements of 8,040 tons (7,294 metric tons). They are 563 feet (172 meters) long and 55 feet (17 meters) wide. Spruance class destroyers carry about 334 people. Their top speed is 33 knots.

Chapter 4

Safety and the Future

Serving on a destroyer is dangerous work. Enemies can damage aluminum destroyers easily. The U.S. Navy makes their newest class of destroyers out of steel. Enemies cannot damage steel as easily as they can damage aluminum. The navy also arms destroyers with powerful new missiles and radar systems. The radar systems use radio waves to locate and guide objects.

The U.S. Navy arms its destroyers with powerful radar systems.

Arleigh Burke Class Destroyers

The navy's newest destroyers belong to the Arleigh Burke class. The navy plans to build 34 ships in this class. Some of these ships are already in service.

Arleigh Burke class destroyers have displacements of about 8,300 tons (7,530 metric tons). They are 466 feet (142 meters) long and 59 feet (18 meters) wide. They carry about 300 people.

Arleigh Burke destroyers are not as fast as some early destroyers. They are made of steel. Steel is heavier than aluminum. Steel adds about 300 tons (272 metric tons) to the displacements of Arleigh Burke class destroyers. The extra weight slows down the destroyers.

Ships of the Arleigh Burke class are guided missile destroyers. They have advanced gun systems that can fire 3,000 bullets per minute. They also carry powerful missiles and advanced radar.

The navy's newest destroyers belong to the Arleigh Burke class.

Missiles

Destroyer crews now rely on missiles more than ever before. Modern missiles allow destroyer crew members to attack enemies from long distances. Destroyer crews are safer from their enemies at long distances.

Destroyer crews use several kinds of missiles. The navy uses Standard missiles against enemy aircraft. Standard missiles are large. They weigh almost 3,000 pounds (1,361 kilograms). Their range is about 100 miles (161 kilometers).

Arleigh Burke class destroyers also carry Tomahawk missiles. Tomahawk missiles are effective against enemies on land. Tomahawk missiles have ranges of about 1,200 miles (1,932 kilometers).

Arleigh Burke destroyers carry Harpoon missiles too. Harpoon missiles are effective at short distances. They have ranges of about 80 miles (129 kilometers). Destroyer crews

Harpoon missiles are effective at short distances.

Destroyer crews that have advanced radar can see enemies approaching early.

use Harpoon missiles mainly against nearby enemy warships.

Radar Systems

Radar helps keep destroyer crews safe. Destroyer crews that have advanced radar can see enemies approaching early. They can prepare for attacks. The crews may be able to escape or call for help.

The newest navy destroyers have the Aegis Anti-Air Warfare System. The Aegis Anti-Air Warfare System is a group of computers and special radar equipment. The system can track as many as 100 objects at once. It checks which objects could be a danger to the ship. This system helps navy commanders know when and where to fire missiles. It also guides these missiles during flight. Systems such as the Aegis Anti-Air Warfare System help keep destroyer crews safer than ever before.

Words to Know

aluminum (uh-LOO-mi-nuhm)—a light, silver-colored metal

armor (AR-mur)—a protective metal covering

depth charge (DEPTH CHARJ)—a metal can filled with explosives

displacement (diss-PLAYSS-muhnt)—the weight of the water a ship pushes away from itself while afloat

escort (ess-KORT)—to travel with and protect

fleet (FLEET)—a group of warships under one command

knot (NOT)—a measurement of speed for ships; one knot equals 1.15 miles (1.85 kilometers) per hour.

launch (LAWNCH)—to set into action

missile (MISS-uhl)—an explosive that can fly long distances

radar (RAY-dar)—machinery that uses radio waves to locate and guide objects

torpedo (tor-PEE-doh)—an explosive that travels underwater

To Learn More

Asimov, Isaac and Elizabeth Kaplan. *How Do Big Ships Float?* Ask Isaac Asimov. Milwaukee: Gareth Stevens, 1993.

Green, Michael. *PT Boats.* Land and Sea. Mankato, Minn.: Capstone Press, 1999.

Green, Michael. *Submarines.* Land and Sea. Mankato, Minn.: Capstone Press, 1998.

Green, Michael. *The United States Navy.* Serving Your Country. Mankato, Minn: Capstone High/Low Books, 1998.

Useful Addresses

Destroyer *Cassin Young*
National Historical Park
Boston, MA 02129

Destroyer *Kidd*
305 South River Road
Baton Rouge, LA 70802

Naval Historical Center
Washington Navy Yard
901 M Street SE
Washington, DC 20374-5060

Internet Sites

Destroyer OnLine Home Page
http://www.plateau.net/usndd

Naval Historical Center
http://www.history.navy.mil

Navy Facts: Destroyers
http://www.chinfo.navy.mil/navpalib/factfile/
  ships/ship-dd.html

U.S. Navy: Welcome Aboard
http://www.navy.mil

Index